FLOYD
ON ITALY

FLOYD
ON ITALY

'I CAME, I SAW, I COOKED!'

'Veni, Vidi, Coxi!'

KEITH FLOYD

Michael Joseph
London

MICHAEL JOSEPH LTD

Published by the Penguin Group
27 Wrights Lane, London W8 5TZ
Viking Penguin Inc., 375 Hudson Street, New York, New York 10014, USA
Penguin Books, Australia Ltd, Ringwood, Victoria, Australia
Penguin Books Canada Ltd, 10 Alcorn Avenue, Toronto, Ontario, Canada M4V 3B2
Penguin Books (NZ) Ltd, 182-190 Wairau Road, Auckland 10, New Zealand

Penguin Books Ltd, Registered Offices: Harmondsworth, Middlesex, England

First published in Great Britain 1994

Copyright © Text Keith Floyd 1994
Copyright © Location photographs Fiona Pragoff
Studio food photographer: Ken Field
Home economist: Karenza Harries
Stylist: Suzie Gittins
Designer: Janet James

Typeset in Galliard
Colour reproduction by Radstock Reproductions Ltd, Midsomer Norton
Printed in England by Butler & Tanner Ltd, Frome and London

A CIP catalogue record for this book is available from the British Library
ISBN 0 7181 3810 4
The moral right of the author has been asserted

ACKNOWLEDGEMENTS

I want to thank Fiona Pragoff not only for taking brilliant pictures, but also for lending a helping hand and mind-reading my moods and needs.

And special thanks to Steve Williams, sadly the only remaining crew member of the original team that made *Floyd on Fish* ten years ago. Without his help with the stove I could not have cooked a thing.

ET TU, PASTA

I hope you will excuse my puerile attempt at Latin translation on the cover of this book, but I think it is funny. Well, nearly funny. My Latin master at school often remarked he'd find it easier to teach the groundsman's cricket pitch roller the rudiments of the language than me.

Anyway, Italian food. What is Italian food? Spaghetti Bolognese, lasagne with coleslaw and deep-pan pizzas filled with assorted culinary garbage? No. A thousand times no. On the subject of pizzas, by the by, in Britain at least they have gone the way of the once noble quiche, which before it got 'wine-barred' and abused was an exquisite dish until, as the late Elizabeth David lamented, it became a culinary dustbin. Whereas thinly rolled dough spread with chopped tomato and topped with anchovies and cheese and zapped into a wood-fired oven is heaven – you just don't need prawns and artichoke hearts, mushroom and chicken tikka pieces in a pastry shell and even if you do you can't call it a pizza.

And do you know, I travelled the length and breadth of Italy without seeing a spaghetti Bolognese on any restaurant menu and definitely not in Bologna? And minestrone soup is not tomato soup with peas and spaghetti hoops.

Let me try and tell you what Italian food really is.

You walk into a restaurant. You sit at a table and ask for a menu. There is no menu, but wine and water are presented at once.

The waiter explains the food available in rapid speak. In Italian. You don't understand. 'Please may I see a menu,' so that with my Penguin dictionary I can work it out. It's hard enough to say please may I see a menu? You tried but he's gone. To a table of happily munching folk who want more. More of what? Leave your table. Walk to theirs, and look.

Oh, wow.

A basket of of fresh broad beans in their shells ripped open and dipped into salt and crunched. Fine thin slivers of (Parma) ham cut from the bone, toasted slices of ciabatta (slipper loaf) drenched in olive oil and rubbed with garlic, a mountain of vibrant red radishes, big green nutty olives as sweet as young hazelnuts. And big glasses of red wine. Then a groaning board of squid and clams and prawns and mussels and octopus, lightly cooked and served cold soused in olive oil and lime or lemon juice (not a drop of balsamic vinegar in sight – it is mainly used in London 'Italian' restaurants, no names, no pack drill – the foodies will know what I mean).

Then a steaming bowl of yellow egg-yolked soft tagliatelle with melted butter, crisp slivers of aged Parmigiano and grated lemon zest. You suck it into your mouth. You smile. You drink. You talk. You laugh. You eat.

They clear the plates, but not the glasses, and bring more wine. They bring lightly grilled lamb chops with oregano and a wedge of lemon.

You almost eat the bones too.

Then a plate of grilled peppers and aubergines. Followed by a soft, succulent wedge of Gorgonzola.

And then you can choose an iceberg of ice creams. With a glass of strega and a tiny cup of strong black coffee.

That is Italian food.

I hope this book will help you to enjoy what I loved.

Keith Floyd
Floyd's Inn (Sometimes)
Tuckenhay, Devon
27 April 1994

CONTENTS

PIEDMONT GARLIC DIP
BAGNA CAUDA

For those who like to remain permanently unsociable, this is a brilliant little recipe for a potent garlic dip from the Piedmont region.

Serves 2–4

100g (4oz) butter
8 tablespoons extra virgin olive oil
100g (4oz) cloves of garlic, very finely sliced
100g (4oz) anchovy fillets, preferably salted ones, but drained canned ones will do
Freshly ground black pepper

TO SERVE
Sliced fresh cardoons or celery; pieces of carrot; chunks of red or green cabbage; slices of roasted or raw red pepper; roasted baby aubergines
Italian country-style bread, such as ciabatta

Melt the butter and olive oil together in a saucepan and add the garlic. Chop up the anchovies and add them to the pan. Cook over a low heat for about 10–15 minutes, stirring whenever you remember, so that you end up with a wonderfully fishy, garlicky sauce. Season to taste. Keep the sauce warm over a spirit lamp, while you dip and dunk into it with fresh raw vegetables like celery, carrots and spring onions, and hunks of crusty Italian bread.

VEGETABLE MINESTRONE
MINESTRONE DI VERDURE

This is one of the great soups of the world. It is a movable feast that has sustained peasants, gourmets and emperors alike since the time of the Borgias (no irony intended here, by the way, it's not poisonous). This is my version, which you can adapt to suit your shopping; just remember freshness is everything. And do buy the best Parmesan and grate it yourself; the pre-grated stuff in packets is dull.

Serves 8–10

4 tablespoons olive oil
2 medium onions, chopped
2 medium carrots, chopped
2 sticks of celery, chopped
450g (1lb) ripe tomatoes, skinned and chopped
2 litres (3 pints) vegetable stock or water
1kg (2¼ lb) broad beans, shelled
450g (1lb) cooked dried beans, such as cannellini beans or flageolets (you could use canned)

450g (1lb) spring cabbage, shredded
100g (4oz) vermicelli, broken into short lengths
Plenty of chopped parsley, flat-leaf if possible
A handful of celery leaves
Salt and freshly ground black pepper
Freshly grated Parmesan cheese, to serve

Heat the olive oil in a very large saucepan, big enough to accommodate all the ingredients. Add the onions, carrots and celery and sauté them for about 10 minutes, until softened. Add the tomatoes and cook for about 5 more minutes, stirring often.

Pour in the stock or water and bring to the boil. Reduce the heat, cover and simmer for 20 minutes or so. Throw in all the remaining ingredients, except for the Parmesan cheese, of course, and cook for about 5–6 more minutes to cook the vermicelli. Check the seasoning, adding a bit more salt and ground black pepper if it is needed.

Ladle into warmed soup bowls and scatter plenty of freshly grated Parmesan over the top. Don't forget some hunks of newly baked ciabatta bread to serve with the soup.

To lie in the Bush under the Southern Cross in the 'Top End' of Australia, wrapped in a swag and fearful of snakes and realizing that man counts for nothing under that awesome sky is a humbling experience. And to pick an olive from a tree that was planted before the Good Samaritan bathed with olive oil the wounds of a man mugged by thugs is another of those extraordinary experiences that I seem to collide with. So to sit before a small wood fire toasting bread and drenching it in olive oil as a mid-morning March snack in a grove of trees where some have been carbon dated to show that they are over two thousand years old and planted before the birth of Christ is weird. To me, anyhow.

The black pearls of the East and
the Mediterranean can be picked
green or left to ripen into black
and knocked from trees into nets.

Salted, stuffed with peppers
or anchovies, spiced with
chillies, preserved in brine or
marinated with olive oil and
diced vegetables or herbs,
what better *amuse-gueules*?

Olive oil: an exceptional and indispensable ingredient for fine cooking and eating. Always buy the best you can afford. It is better in a can or a foil-wrapped bottle because it deteriorates in the sunlight. Use oil within one year of purchase. For the best flavour, buy an extra virgin oil, which comes from the first cold pressings of high grade fruit and has no more than 1 per cent acid. The darker and greener the oil the stronger tasting it will be. Try some single small estate oils if you can. Blends from large producers are cheaper and are more consistent, though the quality of even these varies from year to year. Most of Italy's best oils come from Apulia, Latium, Umbria and Tuscany.

It is a medicament. It is a food. It is good for you. It is the finest cooking oil. And if ever you are planning to hang one on, as they say, a glass before you go on a bender will stop you from suffering the worst excesses of drink. Many a long-lived farmer starts his day with a glass of finest virgin olive oil.

CROSTINI

All self-respecting Italians settle down to a lunch of at least five courses. The first of these, antipasti – that is, the course before the second course, pasta – can be a variety of treats such as slices of salami or cured ham, a dish of nutty fat green olives, grilled or pickled vegetables, anchovy fillets, raw mushrooms in olive oil and lemon juice, hard-boiled eggs with tuna fish mayonnaise – the variety and the list are endless. My favourite, though, is the toasted bread called crostini and bruschetta. Crostini means 'little toasts' and in their simplest form are small, thin pieces of bread brushed with olive oil and toasted; they are sometimes served as croûtons for soup. But they are usually served with puréed spreads. Bruschetta are bigger, thicker pieces of toasted Italian country bread that are sometimes rubbed with a raw clove of garlic, drenched in olive oil and sprinkled with sea salt. (Why don't the Brits esteem and celebrate dripping toast, please?) Often grilled vegetables are used as a topping for bruschetta. Three refined but splendid crostini are as follows.

CROSTINI WITH CALVES' LIVER
CROSTINI CON FEGATI DI VITELLO

Serves 4–6

3 tablespoons olive oil
225g (8oz) calves' liver, chopped
  into tiny cubes
1 very small onion, finely chopped
1 clove of garlic, finely chopped
A good pinch of chopped
  fresh sage

Salt and freshly ground black
  pepper
About 12 small slices of Italian
  country bread (or use French
  bread)
Extra olive oil

Heat the olive oil in a small frying pan and add the calves' liver, frying briskly with the onion, garlic and sage for just a few seconds. Season to taste with salt and pepper. Toast the bread, drizzle with olive oil and top with the liver.

CROSTINI WITH SALT COD
CROSTINI CON BACCALA

Serves 4–6

225g (8oz) plump piece of salt
  cod, soaked overnight
150ml (¼ pint) milk
1 clove of garlic
4–6 tablespoons olive oil

About 12 small slices of Italian
  country bread (or use French
  bread)
Extra olive oil

Drain the salt cod, then rinse it under fresh running water for about 20 minutes. Put it in a shallow pan with the milk and poach it gently for about 20 minutes, until tender. Remove the skin and bones, then flake the fish into morsels.

Pound the garlic clove in a mortar and pestle, then add the fish and pound it down until you have the consistency, if you can imagine, of shreddy mashed potatoes. Now using a jug pour in the olive oil in a thin stream, pounding away at the same time, to give a spreadable purée.

Toast the bread and drizzle with oil, then spread the salt cod purée on top.

CROSTINI WITH ROASTED RED PEPPERS

CROSTINI CON PEPERONI ARROSTO

Serves 4–6

2 red peppers
1 clove of garlic, very finely
 chopped
3 tablespoons olive oil

Salt and freshly ground black pepper
About 12 small slices of Italian
 country bread (or use French
 bread)

Put the peppers into a roasting tin and roast them in a preheated hot oven, 220°C/425°F (gas mark 7), until the skins blacken. You can grill them, turning them often, if you prefer. When the peppers are cool, peel off the skins, cut in half and take out the pith and the pips (taking the pith out of peppers is very important). Chop them finely.

Mix together the garlic and olive oil. Add the peppers and season well with salt and ground black pepper. Leave to marinate for at least an hour.

Toast the bread, drizzle with the marinade and top with the peppers.

United Colours of Italy.

SYMPHONY OF SEAFOOD
ANTIPASTO ALLA MARINARA

This cold hors d'œuvre of mixed shellfish is simplicity itself. But success depends on spanking fresh fish, first-class olive oil and really juicy lemons.

Serves 4–6

3–4 squid
1 octopus
1kg (2¼lb) clams, well-rinsed
450g (1lb) mussels, scrubbed
  (discard any that are damaged
  or remain open when tapped)
Juice of 1 lemon
4 tablespoons extra virgin olive oil

300g (10oz) fresh shell-on
  shrimps or prawns
6–8 fresh shell-on king prawns
Extra lemon juice and olive oil,
  to serve
Salt and freshly ground black
  pepper
Chopped fresh parsley, to serve

Wash and clean the squid and octopus – you can ask your fishmonger to do this for you if you prefer, but it is very easy. Just cut off the tentacles and set them aside, remove the eyes, innards and ink sacs and take out the transparent quill from inside the bodies. Wash away the white fluid. Finally, clean off the skin from the body pouch or 'hood'. Put them into a large pan of cold salted water, bring to the boil, then reduce the heat and simmer for 15 minutes. (Any longer and they will become rubbery.) Drain well and rinse with cold water. Chop into small pieces.

Meanwhile, put the clams and mussels into a saucepan with the lemon juice and the olive oil. Cover and cook for just a few minutes, without adding any other liquid, until they open. Discard any that remain shut. Allow to cool.

To cook the shrimps and prawns, tip them into a pan of lightly salted, furiously boiling water for about 2 minutes, drain well and allow to cool.

Arrange all the seafood on a large serving plate and douse liberally with lemon juice and olive oil. Sprinkle with salt, ground black pepper and plenty of fresh parsley.

LOBSTER AND SCAMPI RISOTTO
RISOTTO DI ARAGUSTA CON SCAMPI

In Northern Italy especially, risotto is a very popular dish and at the first opportunity I ordered one in a restaurant near Milan. What a disappointment it turned out to be. The bowl of slightly sour, undercooked goo covered with congealed grated cheese tasted like half-cooked birdseed – a one-off mistake, I decided. The next day at lunch somewhere in Piedmont, I tried the speciality della casa – risotto with three cheeses. In what appeared to be an elegant, long established, frightfully middle class restaurant, elderly limping waiters in crisp white jackets and black ties served the well-dressed clientele at a leisurely but dignified pace. The clientele were clearly locals, and munching serenely away were a lawyer dining alone, a bishop and whatever a side-kick for a bishop is called, and a sprinkling of ornately coiffured elderly women sitting prim under their pearl-pinned hats. This must be the place for risotto, I thought. However, it was not to be this time either. I received a bowl of gritty gruel and when I asked for the cheese, or rather the three cheeses as advertised, I was coldly informed that the cheese had already been added.

Things were getting out of hand. Where was the famed risotto? Believe it or not, two days later in yet another province, I tried again. This time the rice was cooked although apparently it is supposed to be slightly al dente. So there was only one way out and that was to prepare my own. With the aid of a dictionary, sign language and a smiling lady in a splendid restaurant in Ferrara, somewhere between Parma and Bologna. I discovered a method which I decided to elaborate on, including adding a lobster. So here we go.

LOBSTER AND SCAMPI RISOTTO
RISOTTO DI ARAGUSTA CON SCAMPI

Serves 4

1 live lobster, boiled in water with a glass of wine, a piece of carrot, a few sprigs of parsley and a bay leaf, seasoned with salt and freshly ground black pepper (or buy a lobster that is already cooked)

75g (3oz) butter

1 onion, finely chopped

350g (12oz) Arborio (short-grain) rice

1 wineglass of dry white wine

900ml (1½ pints) fish or chicken stock (preferably from cooking the lobster)

50g (2oz) Parmesan cheese, finely grated

Few strands of saffron

50g (2oz) butter

12–16 fresh scampi (langoustines or Dublin Bay prawns)

Salt and freshly ground black pepper

Juice of 1 lemon

1 wineglass of cognac or grappa

Chopped flat-leaf parsley, to garnish

Thin shavings of Parmesan cheese, to garnish

If using a live lobster, cook it in the boiling water and wine mixture until the shell turns pink, then turn off the heat and allow it to cool. When it is cold, remove the flesh from the lobster, slice it and set aside. Strain the cooking liquid into a jug.

To make the risotto, melt the butter in a large frying pan and sauté the onion for a few minutes until it becomes transparent. Add the rice and cook, stirring, for about 5 minutes. Now add the glass of wine and cook until it has been absorbed by the rice.

Pour in half the stock and bring to the boil. Cover and cook over a very low heat, adding extra stock when necessary, until the rice is just tender. It should be very, very slightly nutty and of a moist, creamy consistency. Keep an eye on it and taste it. It will take about 20 minutes, but as I don't cook with a stopwatch use your common sense. Now add the grated Parmesan and the saffron. Keep hot while you finish the dish.

Heat the remaining butter in a frying pan and quickly sauté the scampi and lobster. Season well with salt, ground black pepper and the lemon juice. Add the glass of cognac or grappa and cook for a minute or so.

Heap the risotto on to warm serving plates. Top with the lobster and scampi mixture, spooning the juices over the top. Scatter with some chopped parsley and the shavings of Parmesan, if you like.

'Sing unto the Lord a new song,
and his praise from the end of
the earth, ye that go down to
the sea, and all that is therein ...'
(Isaiah XLII: 10)

Sailing by.

Calm before the storm.

A labour of love.

Sea urchins are heaven.
Neptune's caviar.

Yum, yum.

Happiness. Freshly caught lake perch, washed and gutted, and grilled over an olive wood fire with sprigs of rosemary, lemon juice, salt and pepper. Country bread. And a glass of red. That's breakfast.

The ones that didn't get away.

FISH BAKED IN SALT

PESCE IN CROSTA

I spent a day wandering round the saltpans near Trapani, Sicily, on a chilly morning watching the windmills rotate eerily in the light breeze.

Salt is so important. A man deemed to be 'worth his salt' was one who sat at the top end of the feudal dinner table. Lesser mortals who sat 'below the salt' were denied the privilege of eating this essential condiment. Some of the best capers I tasted were preserved in salt. Salt cod is an enduring favourite dish of mine. Salted lemons make a smashing side dish for grilled meats. A raw broad bean or a spicy radish dipped in sea salt makes a splendid snack before lunch or dinner with a glass of something chilled. And what of the joys of salt beef and boiled carrots? Or of toothsome cured mountain ham? And where would a new potato be without a sprinkling of the white stuff? I could go on for ever. But the objective here is to introduce a novel way of cooking fish. In salt. Turn immediately to the next page for the recipe.

FISH BAKED IN SALT
PESCE IN CROSTA

Serves 8 or more

2 whole fish, weighing at least
    900g (2lb) each, cleaned and
    scaled (sea bass, sea bream and
    red mullet are good choices –
    one of each would be brilliant)
Sprigs of fresh fennel or dill,
    parsley and basil
Juice of 1 lemon

About 1.4kg (3lb) sea salt
350g (12oz) butter
1 teaspoon hot chilli sauce
Finely grated zest and juice of
    1 large lemon
2 tablespoons chopped fresh
    parsley

Preheat the oven to 220°C/425°F (gas mark 7).

Stuff the cavity of each fish with sprigs of fennel or dill, parsley and basil. Squeeze the lemon juice inside.

Put half the sea salt into a large ovenproof baking dish and place the fish on top. Cover with the remaining salt, packing it around the fish to enclose them completely. Bake in the oven for 20–25 minutes. The salt crust will change colour slightly – the fish will be ready at this point.

While the fish are cooking, mix 100g (4oz) butter with the chilli sauce, beating well to incorporate it. Spoon it on to a piece of foil or greaseproof paper, fold over the foil or paper and roll into a sausage shape. Pop into the freezer to chill thoroughly. Make some flavoured butter in exactly the same way with the grated lemon zest and parsley (mixed together) and another 100g (4oz) of butter.

Crack the salt crust, remove the fish and lay them on a hot serving platter. Keep them in a warm place while you make the lemon butter sauce. Heat the remaining lemon juice in a small saucepan and gradually add small knobs of the rest of the butter, whisking constantly until the butter has melted. Pour over the fish.

Serve at once, with discs of the chilli and lemon parsley butters placed on top of the fish.

RED MULLET WITH PESTO
(PINK FLOYD)
TRIGLIE CON PESTO

We arrived in Vernazza in the Cinque Terre, Liguria, just before sunset. It is a tiny fishing village, very popular with tourists, no doubt because of its stunning beauty. There are brightly painted houses round the edge of the little harbour and dozens of fishing boats bobbing on their moorings. Or rather there should have been. Instead they were berthed high and dry because the weather in late October was too rough for small open boat fishing. This was a bit of a disaster because we had been informed that there would be a plentiful supply of fresh fish at the market the following morning, which would, of course, have been an ideal location for a cooking sketch. However, the wind was so strong you could barely stand and if you could cling on you were drenched by the foaming white spray blowing off the sea. An exhaustive search of the few shops that there were, and the local restaurant, gave us no hope of finding the ingredients we needed. So we had to move on further down the coast. I stuck a pin in the map and chose Monterosso.

To save time we took the mountain coast road. We left the village and climbed hundreds of feet above the ocean. On this fine Sunday morning the view of the dramatic Ligurian coastline was quite breathtaking. But I suffer from vertigo and could not bear to look down and by now, to make matters worse, the road had turned into a stony, muddy, rutted cart-track running along the very edge of the mountain without barriers of any kind.

We were still climbing higher and higher and the track surface continued to deteriorate. My knuckles were white on the wheel and I felt physically sick so I stopped the car. There was no possibility of turning and retracing our steps so we had no choice but to go on. It took nearly two hours to cover what could not have been more than 10 miles. Monterosso was just waking when we arrived and, blessed relief, a café was opening. We gulped down strong coffees with brandies and munched on gooey chocolate cake – it was heaven. It is a pretty village, not as striking as Vernazza but it has a more workaday atmosphere – it has shops, a couple of fish stalls, a delightful bar

where we breakfasted on slivers of Parmigiano and Parma ham, washed down with a very agreeable red Cinque Terre DOC to the strains of wonderfully romantic Italian dance bands from the forties and fifties.

Much fortified by yet more coffee and brandy, we started to explore the town and quickly made friends with the owner of a great little restaurant called Ciak, just by the church. He provided the ingredients and gave us all manner of generous (typically Italian) assistance. So under the curious gazes of the locals coming out of church, I set up my kitchen in the main street and prepared this little dish, which we call Pink Floyd because my wife's maiden name was mullet and the principal ingredient of this dish is red mullet. Needless to say, practically any fish can be used.

RED MULLET WITH PESTO (PINK FLOYD)
TRIGLIE CON PESTO

Serves 4

FOR THE PESTO SAUCE
2–3 cloves of garlic
50g (2oz) pine nuts
1 large bunch of fresh basil
1 large bunch of fresh parsley,
    flat-leaf if possible
About 6 tablespoons olive oil
350g (12oz) fresh pasta, such
    as tagliatelle, fettucine
2 tablespoons olive oil
Good pinch of salt

4 red mullet, cleaned and scaled
4 tablespoons olive oil
Good squeeze of lemon juice
25g (1oz) pine nuts
4 tomatoes, skinned, seeded and
    chopped
1 tablespoon each chopped
    fresh basil and parsley, flat-leaf
    if possible
Salt and freshly ground black
    pepper
2 lemons, halved, to serve

First make the pesto sauce by pounding together the garlic and pine nuts in a mortar and pestle. Tear the basil and parsley leaves from their stalks and add them to the mixture, pounding them down well. Slowly drizzle in the olive oil and mix until well blended. All this can be done in a food processor or blender if you want to save time. The pesto should look like a thickish mint sauce.

Put a big pan of water on to cook the pasta, adding the olive oil and a good pinch of salt to flavour it. When the water is boiling, add the pasta and cook until just tender – al dente.

Meanwhile, fry the mullet in 3 tablespoons of oil for about 7 minutes, turning it over once and adding a good squeeze of lemon juice to flavour it. Add the pine nuts and tomatoes to the pan, then transfer the fish to warm serving plates.

Finish off the sauté of tomatoes and pine nuts by adding the chopped basil and parsley. Season with salt and ground black pepper and add the extra tablespoon of olive oil. Pour this around the fish and serve with the cooked pasta. Spoon the pesto sauce on top of the fish and serve with the lemon halves.

Rooms with views.

ITALIAN FISH STEW
BURRIDA

And while we are on the subject of simple but good things, here's another – the Italian fish soup called *Burrida*. Now this is not the meal to cook on a whim one wet Saturday afternoon for that evening's dinner party. Anyway, in my view it is a lunch dish. No, this should be a soup you feel inspired to make after an exhilarating stroll around a busy fish market on a warm summer's day. You will need probably one or two kilos of strong-flavoured, firm-fleshed fish like eel, monkfish, octopus, red snapper, large prawns, dogfish, etc., etc. – you only make this soup for a minimum of six people.

Serves 6–8

90ml (3fl oz) olive oil
1 small onion, finely chopped
1 small carrot, finely diced
2 sticks of celery, finely chopped
1kg (2¼ lb) ripe plum tomatoes, skinned, seeded and chopped
3–4 anchovy fillets, chopped (optional)
1 tablespoon chopped fresh basil
1 tablespoon chopped fresh parsley, flat-leaf, if possible
2–3 cloves of garlic, finely chopped

Salt and freshly ground black pepper
1.5 litres (2½ pints) hot water
2kg (4½ lb) firm-fleshed fish, filleted and cut into large pieces (choose from a mixture of eels, monkfish, squid, octopus, scampi tails, red snapper, etc.) – ask your fishmonger to prepare it for you
Chopped fresh basil and parsley, to garnish

Heat the oil in a very large saucepan or flameproof casserole and sauté the onion for about 3–4 minutes until lightly browned. Add the carrot and celery and sauté for a few more minutes, then add the tomatoes and anchovies, if using. Stir well, then add the basil, parsley and garlic. Season with salt and ground black pepper. Pour in the hot water and bring to the boil.

If you are using octopus or squid, add to the pan, put the lid on and cook for about 25 minutes before adding the rest of the fish, then cook for about 20 more minutes once that has been added to the pot.

Ladle the stew into warmed bowls and garnish with the basil and parsley.

The signature fish of Italy.
Scampi. But it probably came
from Scotland.

And now the corny caption.
Man selling guinea fowl at
Orvieto market.

Some days there ain't no fish –
Hoagy Carmichael.
Fish is my favourite dish –
Fats Waller.
You're like a one-eyed cat
sleeping in a seafood store –
Elvis Presley.
Jambalaya crawfish pie and
filé gumbo –
Fats Domino.
Our soles are cheap today.
Cheaper than yesterday. (Trad.
Anon. but performed by Bath
RFC to the tune of *La Traviata*.)

So if you will pardon the outrageous cliché, nay schoolboy
pun. If music be the food of
love, play on.
But not all references to fish in
some songs referred to here have
anything to do with cooking or
eating. Anyway, this is a family
foodie book so I won't dwell on
THAT subject.
Suffice to say I would (and you
probably think I'm philistine)
rather spend an hour in a fish
market than a day at the Uffizi.

COUSCOUS WITH FISH SAUCE AND LOBSTER OR CRAYFISH

COUSCOUS CON SALSA DI PESCE E ARAGOSTA

After many weeks on the road travelling through Italy with my trusty portable stove and a film crew I was getting bored of veal steaks and a wedge of lemon, bored of (increasingly poor quality as we travelled south) pasta and sick to the back teeth of small bony fish, squid or octopus. I craved vegetables, soups, lamb chops. So imagine my joy as I sped along the twisting roads of Sicily and saw the rugged hills and mountains alive with grazing sheep. Lamb chops at last. And maybe even some potatoes.

But no. Fish, pasta and veal steaks again. Indeed, the restaurant in my hotel didn't even open on Saturday and Sunday nights, so back to the grotty trattorias in Trapani. But. But. There was a light at the end of the gastronomic tunnel. Sicily is close to Tunisia. And joy. Because the Tunisians who live in Sicily have brought couscous to the island. Not to eat with chicken, carrots and merguez as in Provence, but with fish and fish sauce. Turn to the next page for my version.

Chillies, another North African contribution to Sicilian cuisine.

COUSCOUS WITH FISH SAUCE AND LOBSTER OR CRAYFISH

COUSCOUS CON SALSA DI PESCE E ARAGOSTA

Serves 4–6

4 tablespoons olive oil
2 medium onions, finely chopped
2 sticks of celery, chopped
2 cloves of garlic, crushed
450g (1lb) ripe tomatoes, skinned
  and chopped
A handful of chopped fresh
  parsley
A handful of chopped fresh fennel
  or dill
2 bay leaves
About 2 litres (3 pints) water
About 1kg (2¼ lb) firm-fleshed
  fish (choose from a mixture of

red snapper, grey mullet, sea
  bream, monkfish, hake, eels,
  etc.), cleaned, skinned and cut
  into chunks
225g (8oz) couscous
1 cooked lobster, cut in half
  (see the recipe for Lobster and
  Scampi Risotto on page 30 if
  you want to cook a live lobster)
Salt and freshly ground black
  pepper
Juice of 1 lemon
50g (2oz) butter
Hot chilli paste (harissa) to serve

Heat the olive oil in a very large saucepan and add the onions, celery and garlic. Sweat them down with the lid on for about 5 minutes, but don't let them go brown. Add the tomatoes, parsley, fennel or dill and bay leaves and cook over a low heat for about 15 minutes, adding an extra slosh of olive oil if necessary. Now add the water and bring it up to the boil. Reduce the heat so that the water is just simmering, then add the fish. Cover and cook very gently for about 15–20 minutes.

Use a ladle to strain off about half a litre of this fish broth (a little less than 1 pint) to use for the couscous. Transfer the remaining broth, including all the fish, vegetables and herbs, apart from the bay leaves, to a liquidiser or food processor, in batches, if necessary. Process until smooth, then strain through a fine sieve and season to taste. Return to the pan and keep hot.

Now prepare the couscous, following the instructions on the packet, but instead of using water, use the reserved fish broth. (Not the liquidised soup.) Meanwhile, put the lobster on the grill rack and squeeze the juice of a lemon over it, then add a few knobs of butter. Place it under a very hot grill and cook for about 6–8 minutes, then divide the flesh into large chunks.

Pile the cooked couscous on to a hot serving dish and place the lobster pieces on top. Serve the fish soup alongside, for spooning over the couscous and lobster, little by little. A hot chilli paste is a good accompaniment.

Need some dough, Joe?

A tired, hardworking baker had one day baked and sold his bread and looked into his basket for a snack. Alas, he had left it at home and, hands on hips, like frustrated and angry people do, he stood pondering his hungry fate. He espied a morsel of dough too small to make a loaf. His wood oven was still hot and outside the early morning world had woken and stallholders were setting out their produce in the market.

He bought a slice of ham and a wedge of cheese, pinched a couple of capers and some tomato from a fellow artisan and returned to his bakery. And in a blinding flash of inspiration, he rolled out his dough into a thin sheet and placed the ham, tomato and slivers of cheese on it and popped it into the oven.

The thin dough cooked
quickly in the dying embers.
The cheese melted and the ham
sizzled. He sprinkled on the
salted capers and ate his hot
concoction, rather like a slice of
Yorkshire pudding, munching
happily away.
The pizza was created. And
became world famous.
Until the late-twentieth century
when it suffered the fate of
the once prestigious quiche. If
Giovanni Costello walked into
an American deep-pan pizza
shop and saw the pastry tart that
took its name from his innova-
tive breakfast 220 years ago he
would be devastated.

It takes years to flip it out like
this. So don't practise for your
first dinner party. Just roll it out
with a pin or bottle.

Toppings are what you fancy. My favourite is cheese, tomato, anchovy and caper. But as long as you have a chopped or puréed tomato base you can add what you like – salami, mushrooms, ham etc., etc. – but please don't turn it into a 'culinary dustbin'.

PIZZA

Serves 4

FOR THE DOUGH
450g (1lb) plain flour
25g (1oz) fresh yeast, dissolved
   in a little warm water
1 teaspoon salt
About 300ml (½ pint) hand-hot
   water

Sift the flour on to a work surface and make a well in the middle. Pour the dissolved yeast into the well, then add the salt and mix together. Bit by bit add the warm water, kneading all the time until you get a soft-textured, pliable dough. You can use an electric beater for this if you prefer. Knead the dough until it is light and elastic, then form it into four balls. Put them on to floured plates, cover and leave in a warm place for about an hour to rise.

Roll out the balls of dough into circles about 30cm (12 inches) in diameter. Drizzle a little olive oil over the surface and top with sliced onions, chopped tomatoes, sliced mushrooms, Mozzarella cheese, salami, chopped garlic, chopped oregano or parsley in whatever combination you like.

When cooking in a wood-fired brick oven the pizzas take about 6–7 minutes to cook. At home, bake them in the oven at its highest temperature on a flat metal baking tray that you will have pre-heated, so that the base cooks crisply. They will take about 12–15 minutes.

PASTA

My first experience of pasta was in the late fifties in a coffee bar in Bristol. It was a dish called Spaghetti Bolognese – a mountain of spaghetti with a tomato-flavoured, minced meat sauce topped with melted Cheddar cheese. I was wildly impressed by this meal – it cost, I think, about one shilling and nine pence – so I scoured the Bristol shops for spaghetti to cook at home and was amazed and baffled to discover it came in dried sticks in a blue paper packet.

Problem. How to get the stuff into the saucepan without breaking it (it had been in long pieces at the coffee bar). Did I soak it first or what? My mother's Mrs Beeton was no help. And Mum didn't know either. Eventually, I phoned the restaurant and asked. Simple – you fed the sticks into rapidly boiling water as they softened. Terrific. I made my sauce with mince and a tin of tomatoes and declared myself a cook … I was sixteen and working as a cub reporter on the *Bristol Evening Post*. But the seed was sown.

In the intervening years I have eaten Spaghetti Bolognese many, many times in countless restaurants around the world. But it was not until I visited Italy in general and Bologna in particular that I discovered there is no such dish as Spaghetti Bolognese. Also, I discovered that Marco Polo did not introduce pasta from his voyages to China – the Italians were eating pasta long before. Pasta – spaghetti or tagliatelle or whatever – served with a meat sauce is called *Spaghetti al Ragù*! So there. (Incidentally, there is no such dish as Chop Suey in the Chinese kitchen either.)

Dried pasta is very acceptable but freshly made stuff with fine durum flour, eggs and olive oil is spectacular and it is well worth the time and trouble to make your own. If you can afford it, buy a pasta machine so you can make all the different shapes and sizes.

First, though, it is important to know how to make the basic dough, then you can decide what shapes you want to make. The way we do it at Floyd's Inn is as follows.

On a worktop mix with your hands approximately 350g (12oz) Italian soft wheat flour (known as type 'OO'), or just use plain white flour, with two egg yolks, a dash of olive oil and a good pinch of salt, until you have a tacky dough. Now add two or three whole beaten eggs and continue kneading until you have a smooth, pliable dough.

Cover and leave it to rest for a good half hour. Then roll it out on a floured surface and cut it to the required size. This is where the pasta machine comes in handy, because cutting, or indeed as I have in Italy, hand-rolling spaghetti is a laborious affair.

You can flavour the pasta with tomato purée, spinach purée or squid ink, which not only flavours the stuff but gives a pleasing choice of colours – yellow 'au naturel', pink, green or black.

Anyway, here are three of my favourite recipes:

SPAGHETTI (OR TAGLIATELLE) WITH MEAT SAUCE

SPAGHETTI (O TAGLIATELLE) AL RAGÙ

Chop some good beef into very fine dice – don't mince it. Fry some very finely chopped onion in 3 or 4 tablespoons of olive oil with some crushed garlic. When these are soft and transparent add the meat and a load of tomatoes, which have been skinned, seeded and finely chopped. Season with salt and pepper and a sprig of fresh thyme, oregano or sage, or a pinch of dried and simmer for 30–40 minutes, till you have a glistening rich red sauce.

As this is coming to an end pop some fresh pasta into boiling salted water – it will take a couple of minutes only. Drain well, put it into bowls and add a bit of the meat *ragù*. And do sprinkle some freshly grated Parmesan cheese over it. It is better than the Spaghetti Bolognese I first cooked nearly thirty-four years ago. But not as good as the dishes I tasted in Ferrara's Central Restaurant. Next time you are passing, try it. I had the best food there in my whole trip.

TAGLIATELLE
WITH SCALLOPS AND BEANS
TAGLIATELLE CON CANESTRELLI E FAGIOLI

There is a town in Apulia, south-east Italy, called Noci. It is a few kilometres from the coast, a coast of formerly picturesque fishing villages, now vandalized by hideous modern development. In late March when I was there the almond and cherry trees were beginning to blossom. The vineyards were neatly ploughed. The olive groves glinted lead-green in the sun. On the coast you ate fish. Mainly octopus, squid, clams and a myriad of small bony fish indifferently deep-fried or grilled. And in the hills (and Noci) you ate tough, eggless, ear-shaped pasta with boiled turnip greens. *Orecchiette alla Verza* or something like that. It was horrible. But esteemed by the locals as a very special dish.

The dullness of the food in that region was odd, because the markets were full of fine fresh produce yet it did not appear on the table of any restaurant that I visited. Everything was pasta and turnip greens or fried fish.

How was I going to reflect the region gastronomically for this book and my television programme with so little inspiration?

I set up my portable kitchen in the middle of Noci's very busy market and went shopping. I found fresh pasta, new season's broad beans, crunchy spinach, succulent scallops and sweet lemons and I joined Italy and Asia together by creating this half-Mediterranean, half-Chinese dish.

TAGLIATELLE WITH SCALLOPS AND BEANS
TAGLIATELLE CON CANESTRELLI E FAGIOLI

Serves 4

3 tablespoons olive oil
About 50g (2oz) fatty Parma
  ham, diced into small cubes
450g (1lb) fresh tagliatelle
Salt
1kg (2¼ lb) fresh young broad
  beans, shelled
12–16 scallops (depending on
  their size), removed from their
shells and washed, or use about
  450g (1lb) large shelled prawns
Freshly ground black pepper
Juice of ½ lemon
100g (4oz) rocket or young
  spinach leaves, rinsed
75g (3oz) cherry tomatoes,
  quartered

Heat 2 tablespoons of the olive oil in a large frying pan or wok. Add the cubes of ham, which give a great flavour to this little dish, and fry them until crispy. In the meantime, bring a big pan of lightly salted water up to the boil for the pasta. Add the tagliatelle and cook it for 4–5 minutes, until it is just tender – al dente.

While the pasta is cooking, add the broad beans and scallops or prawns to the hot fat and stir-fry them briskly for 2–3 minutes (the scallops should just be opaque). Season with salt, ground black pepper and lemon juice. Use a slotted spoon to remove the beans and scallops (or prawns) from the pan and keep warm.

Heat the remaining olive oil in the frying pan or wok and add the rocket or spinach, stir-frying it over a high heat for a few moments. Return the beans and scallops or prawns to the pan to heat them through. Drain the pasta and put it into a warm serving dish. Tip the bean mixture over the top and serve at once, scattered with the cherry tomatoes.

RAVIOLI WITH SPINACH AND RICOTTA FILLING
RAVIOLI RIPIENI DI RICOTTA E SPINACI

Serves 4

FOR THE FRESH PASTA DOUGH
350g (12oz) strong plain flour
Good pinch of salt
Few drops of olive oil
3 eggs (size 3 or 4)
FOR THE FILLING
225g (8oz) fresh spinach,
    well washed and trimmed
A knob or two of butter

100g (4oz) Ricotta cheese
2 eggs, separated
50g (2oz) freshly grated
    Parmesan cheese
Good pinch of freshly grated
    nutmeg
Salt and freshly ground black
    pepper
50g (2oz) butter, melted

First, make the pasta dough. Sift the flour and salt into a mound on your work surface – marble is perfect because it keeps cool. Make a well in the middle, add the olive oil and break in the eggs. Draw in the flour with your hands and mix to form a stiff paste – you may need to add a little extra flour. Wash your hands and clean the work top, then sprinkle both with a little flour. Knead the dough for about 10 minutes until it is smooth and elastic. Wrap, chill and rest for half an hour.

To make the filling, cook the spinach in a large pan with some butter for a few minutes, drain well, cool a little, then wring out the excess water with your hands. Chop and mix with the Ricotta cheese, egg yolks (reserve the whites) and half the Parmesan cheese. Season with nutmeg, salt and ground black pepper.

Roll out the pasta dough thinly on a lightly floured surface to make two sheets measuring about 40 x 25cm (16 x 10 inches). Place small spoonfuls of the filling on top of one piece of pasta in neat rows, leaving space around each little mound. Brush the pasta with lightly beaten reserved egg white, then position the second piece of pasta on top. Press gently to exclude the air, then press down firmly to seal. Use a pastry wheel with a fluted edge to cut the pasta into small filled ravioli parcels.

Bring a large pan of salted water to the boil, carefully slide in the ravioli and cook for 3–4 minutes, hoping that they don't fall apart, like mine did. Dish them up on to a warmed serving plate, drizzle with melted butter and season with salt, pepper, more freshly grated nutmeg and plenty of Parmesan, or serve with fresh tomato sauce (see page 82).

WALNUT SAUCE

Serves 4

This rich sauce is served with ribbon pasta in Italy: tagliatelle, fettucine, pappardelle or linguine. It would also go well with grilled chicken or white fish, or with a dish of baked mushrooms or roasted vegetables, such as peppers, fennel or leeks.

In a food processor or blender grind 50g (2oz) shelled walnuts until fairly fine but not powdered (the sauce is best a little crunchy). Melt 25g (1oz) butter with 1 tablespoon extra virgin olive oil in a saucepan. Stir in the ground nuts, then add 225ml (8fl oz) double cream. Season to taste with salt and freshly ground black pepper. Bring just to the boil, then lower the heat and simmer for about 2 minutes, until thickened.

Taste of success.
Fresh vegetables naturally grown under a hot sun give a unique flavour to the simplest of dishes.

A favourite antipasto is a plate of grilled vegetables. Simply slice some aubergines and courgettes. Cut a couple of tomatoes in half. Cut some red and green peppers into rectangles. Arrange the vegetables in a single layer in an olive-oiled, flameproof baking tin or dish. Souse the vegetables liberally with olive oil and pop the tin directly under a preheated hot grill for about 5 minutes, or until the vegetables begin to brown. Turn the slices over with a spatula, brush with more olive oil, and put the tin back under the grill. Cook for another 3–4 minutes. Serve with more olive oil and sprinkle with ground sea salt.

TUSCANY COURGETTES AND MUSHROOMS

Serves 4–6

Heat 3 tablespoons of olive oil and 50g (2oz) butter in a large frying pan. Add 225g (8oz) sliced button mushrooms, and sauté briskly for 3–4 minutes. Turn down the heat. Add 3 cloves of garlic to the pan, together with a tablespoon of chopped fresh mint. Cover and cook for 10 minutes. Add 450g (1lb) sliced courgettes to the pan. Cover and cook for 10 minutes more. Season with salt and black pepper. Remove the garlic cloves and serve.

PASTA WITH FRESH HERBS

Serves 4

This is one of the quickest dishes to make. Bring a large pan of water to a boil over high heat. Melt a little butter and a couple of tablespoons olive oil in a pan, add a chopped clove of garlic and cook for about 2–3 minutes. Then add about 50g (2oz) fresh chopped herbs. Use about half flat-leaf parsley and half a mixture of, say, basil, marjoram, chives, mint, coriander, oregano, lovage – whatever you have.

The butter and oil must not be hot enough to cook the herbs, only to heat through and soften them. You could also add some chopped lemon zest and pine nuts. Meanwhile, add salt and fresh pasta (see page 67) to the pan and cook for about 3–5 minutes. Drain and toss well with the herb sauce. Season with salt and ground black pepper and serve at once with freshly grated Parmesan cheese.

FRESH TOMATO SAUCE

Makes about 300ml (¹/₂ pint)

Heat 4 tablespoons of extra virgin olive oil in a large, heavy-based saucepan. Add 1 finely chopped onion and fry for about 3–4 minutes until it is transparent, then add a large crushed clove of garlic, 1kg (2¼ lb) very ripe plum tomatoes, skinned, seeded and chopped, 1 tablespoon of chopped fresh basil, 1 teaspoon of caster sugar, a few drops of wine vinegar and some salt and freshly ground black pepper. Simmer slowly for as long as it takes to get a rich, thick, red sauce.

And now abideth three things
Tomatoes, Basil and Olives:
The Italian trinity.

FLOYD'S INN ITALIAN-STYLE VEGETABLE ANTIPASTI

Tired? Jaded? Tastebuds blunted by red meat, rich sauces? Bored with over-complicated food? You are? So sometimes am I. And the perfect solution is this:

First, cook some globe artichokes in plenty of boiling salted water until an outside leaf comes away easily when you pull it. This usually takes at least 30 minutes. Drain and cool. Remove the hearts, discarding the leaves and scraping out the hairy 'chokes'. Slice the hearts. Second, braise 3 or 4 heads of chicory (white endive) in home-made chicken stock. Strain, cool and slice in half (reserve the stock, because by adding some vermicelli to it you can have an excellent light soup for lunch tomorrow).

Now prepare a large baking tray for grilling the vegetables and place on it: some slices of cored and seeded red and green peppers, some thin slices of aubergine, the braised chicory and the sliced artichoke hearts. Drizzle the lot with olive oil and sprinkle with a little garlic, lemon juice, salt and freshly ground pepper. Pop the lot under a hot grill until it is all golden and scrumptious. Garnish with chopped anchovy fillets and parsley.

Serve with toasted slices of country bread soaked in olive oil and rubbed with garlic.

I am recommending this as a meal in itself, but, of course, in Italy it could well be the first of a five-course meal, including pasta, meat or fish, cheese, dessert or fruit.

Bargaining for fish and
fishing for bargains.

POT-ROASTED PIGEONS, CHIANTI-STYLE
PICCIONI AL CHIANTI

Wearing a pair of yellow gloves, a natty English suit, a silk scarf and a straw hat (with Lonnie Donegan on my mind), I sped through the vine-clad slopes of the Chianti in a convertible Aston Martin – except James Bond would have had a metallic brown one – to a sleepy town called Castellina in Chianti. Through narrow streets of closed shops I arrived in the church square to find a stunning silence; just a huge blue sky with a few big blackbirds swooping through the illuminated church tower. A *carabiniere* was strolling to lunch.

The door of the car slammed with a gentle 'plop' and the only sound in the square was the 'click' of my leather-soled suede shoes. A soft hot wind was blowing as I stepped through the door of the Trattoria La Torre. The contrast between the tranquillity of the church square and the noisy clattering of hungry Italians crunching, munching, chewing, slurping, talking, laughing, gesticulating was dramatic. The place was packed. Because I am a very privileged person I was swept with gracious courtesy into the kitchen where the bulky senior *cuoco* was orchestrating the efforts of half-a-dozen white-overalled, benign, smiling women, who were chopping, roasting, grilling and stirring over fiercely burning gas rings and volcanic wood-fuelled grills.

Despite their age and size they moved with the grace of ballerinas arranging on plates exquisite food from massive cold rooms or blackened roasting trays. Luigi, as I now know him to be, head chef, author and gentleman, suggested a very young Chianti Classico voluptuous fruity red to drink while he prepared my lunch. It was the first time I had drunk Chianti since it was considered a much maligned liquid involving banana skins in the late fifties and early sixties but it was truly a delight. While I was nibbling on a selection of grilled veg delicately perfumed with extra virgin olive oil and balsamic, asthmatic whatever it is vinegar, my chum Luigi was preparing two plump pigeons that would arrive upon a bed of risotto, which was cooked with red wine. I returned the following day to the same church square and, under the bemused eyes of the *carabiniere*, postman and a nun on a bicycle, I attempted to recreate Luigi's Pot-roasted Pigeons, Chianti-style.

POT-ROASTED PIGEONS, CHIANTI-STYLE
PICCIONI AL CHIANTI

Serves 4

4 pigeons
A handful of fresh sage
Salt and freshly ground black
    pepper
4 tablespoons olive oil
1 onion, finely chopped
1 stick of celery, finely chopped
2 cloves of garlic, finely chopped
600ml (1 pint) pigeon, chicken or
    game stock

2 wineglasses of Chianti Classico
2 tablespoons tomato purée
100g (4oz) pigeon or chicken
    livers, finely chopped
225g (8oz) Arborio
    (short-grain) rice
50g (2oz) butter
50g (2oz) hard sheep's cheese,
    such as Pecorino Romano
    or Sardo

Stuff the pigeons with sage and season all over with salt and pepper. Heat the oil in a large flameproof casserole and brown the birds. Next add the onion. Cook for a couple of minutes, then stir in the celery and garlic. Add most of the stock, the wine, tomato purée and pigeon or chicken livers. Allow the wine to evaporate a little, then cover and simmer over a low heat for about 45 minutes, until the birds are tender.

Transfer the pigeons to another cooking pot with a couple of spoonfuls of the sauce. Cover and simmer very gently to keep warm. Stir the rice into the remaining sauce and cook until the liquid has been absorbed, about 12–15 minutes. Add a little more stock if necessary. The rice should be moist and tender, but very slightly nutty.

Stir the butter into the rice and let it melt, then add the cheese. Heap this risotto on to warm serving plates and lift the pigeons on top. Pour over the sauce.

FRESH GARDEN PEAS, SICILIAN-STYLE
PISELLI ALLA SICILIANA

This is a simple but superb way to celebrate fresh garden peas. It is important to realise that the peas are the main event. The strips of chicken can be just for flavouring. As often happened on my journey through Italy, I was stuck for inspiration until I saw mountains of peas in the local market. Bright green, fresh and crunchy, piled as high as small hayricks or spilling from the back of one of those pale green, three-wheeled trucks that abound. I was on the little island of Marettimo, an hour or so from the west coast of Sicily by hydrofoil, to film the Festival of St Joseph, where a young girl and boy playing the part of Mary and Joseph attempt to enter the church. Three times they are refused but on the fourth occasion they are admitted. Everybody cheers. The church bells ring and the priest leads the assembled villagers, flanked by Mary and Joseph, to a communal feast in the village square. Where they all get a little sozzled and dance and sing. It's great fun. While they were thus cavorting, I cooked this dish of peas, much to the amusement of the assembled revellers.

Serves 4

2 tablespoons olive oil
50g (2oz) butter
1 bunch of spring onions, trimmed and chopped
2 carrots, chopped into small dice
1 thick slice of prosciutto ham, cut into small cubes
2 boned chicken breasts, sliced into 1.5cm (½ inch) strips

Salt
1 or 2 wineglasses of dry white wine
1kg (2¼ lb) fresh peas, shelled
150ml (5fl oz) milk
A handful of chopped fresh oregano
Freshly ground black pepper

Heat the olive oil and butter in a large frying pan. Add the spring onions, carrots and prosciutto, sautéing for about 5 minutes, until softened. Add the strips of chicken to the pan, season with a little salt and fry until golden.
Pour in the wine and bubble it up until it has evaporated. Remove the chicken from the pan with a slotted spoon and keep in a warm place. Add the peas to the frying pan and cook over a gentle heat for about 5 minutes. Return the chicken to the pan, stir in the milk and oregano and cook for 10 more minutes. Season to taste with salt and ground black pepper, then serve immediately.

WHITE BEAN GOULASH
GOULASH DI FAGIOLI

I adore pulses of any kind. A soothing Indian dal, a warming green pea and ham soup. Or a plate of mushy peas; a slab of pease pudding; braised lentils; a salad of white haricot beans and tuna fish tossed in lemon juice and olive oil with chopped onions. Or boiled ham with parsley sauce and butter beans. Or a wonderful *soupe au pistou* enriched with dried red beans. Not to mention a serious chilli con carne (heavy on the chillies and beans, light on the meat).

This delightful dish of dried white beans is a simple country recipe, the ingredients of which any self-respecting farmhouse would have permanently in its larder. Paprika or dried chillies, the meaty bone from a mountain-air cured ham, garlands of garlic, a barrel of olive oil and, of course, a sack of dried beans. But it is that kind of dish. You don't cook it until you have eaten all the prosciutto (ham), which will have taken weeks of lunches. It is a dish to do with good housekeeping. It is the essence of resourcefulness, so necessary to good eating. It is also very tasty, nutritious, filling and economical. Ho. Ho. Try it.

WHITE BEAN GOULASH
GOULASH DI FAGIOLI

Serves 4–6

450g (1lb) dried flageolet beans
(or use cannellini beans),
soaked overnight
2 litres (3 pints) water
1 ham bone (even better –
1 Parma ham bone)
1 carrot, finely chopped
1 large onion, finely chopped
2 cloves of garlic, chopped
1 sprig of fresh thyme
1 bay leaf

1 sprig of fresh parsley
Salt
3 tablespoons olive oil
1 teaspoon mild paprika
1/2 teaspoon hot paprika
2 tablespoons chopped flat-leaf
parsley
2 tablespoons white wine vinegar
150ml (5fl oz) soured cream
Chopped fresh chives, to garnish

Rinse the soaked beans in plenty of fresh water, then put them into a very large saucepan with the water. Bring up to boiling point and boil rapidly for 10 minutes. (It is a good idea to do this with all dried beans as some of them contain toxins that need to be destroyed.)

Put the ham bone into the saucepan with the beans and add the carrot, half the onion, 1 clove of garlic, the thyme, bay leaf and parsley. Cover and simmer over a low heat for 1 1/2 –2 hours, until the beans are really tender. Season with salt about halfway through the cooking time – it is unlikely that you will need much, if any, because of the saltiness of the ham bone.

When the beans are cooked, remove the bone, bay leaf and thyme. Shred any meat from the bone that hasn't already fallen off and add it back to the saucepan.

Heat the olive oil in a frying pan and gently fry the remaining onion and garlic for about 5 minutes, until softened. Add the mild and hot paprika and sauté for 2 more minutes. Sir into the saucepan with the chopped parsley and vinegar and cook for 10 minutes. Season with salt and more paprika, if necessary.

Ladle into bowls, spoon some soured cream on top and sprinkle with chopped chives.

Two Italian classics, one sweet, one savoury, using lemon as a main ingredient, are Veal *Scaloppine* (Escalopes) in Lemon Sauce, and Lemon *Granita* (Water Ice). The veal dish is incredibly quick and easy to prepare. The *granita* (different from a sorbet in using fresh fruit juice rather than a purée as its base) is wonderfully refreshing at any time on a hot Italian day.

VEAL *SCALOPPINE* IN LEMON SAUCE

Serves 4

Dust 4 beaten-out escalopes of veal, each weighing about 100g (4oz), with flour seasoned with salt and freshly ground black pepper. Heat 1 tablespoon olive oil with 25g (1oz) butter and when foaming add the escalopes. Fry quickly (about 30 seconds on each side, which is why the escalopes need to be beaten out thin). Remove from the pan and keep warm. Off the heat, add 2 tablespoons fresh lemon juice and the grated zest of 1 lemon to the pan, together with 15g (½ oz) butter and salt and pepper. Heat until the butter is melted, then add 2 tablespoons finely chopped parsley. Return the veal to the pan and heat through. Serve at once, garnished with lemon slices.

LEMON *GRANITA*

Serves 4

Make a sugar syrup by dissolving 350g (12oz) granulated sugar in 175ml (6fl oz) water in a heavy-based saucepan over a moderate heat. Stir constantly while the sugar dissolves, then boil briskly for 2–3 minutes. Leave to cool completely, then add 225ml (8floz) fresh lemon juice, for which you will need about 8 large lemons: when you squeeze them, extract as much of the fruit pulp as possible, and add to the syrup as well. Stir thoroughly, pour into a bowl and freeze for 3–4 hours, stirring the mixture once every hour, until it is slushy. Whizz in a blender or food processor until frothy and smooth, then return to the bowl, cover and freeze for a further 1–2 hours, until firm.

And the flowers are so sweet
But the fruit of the poor lemon
is impossible to eat.
(Peter, Paul and Mary)

But they are wrong.
Sicilian lemons are superb.

HUNTER'S RABBIT
CONIGLIO ALLA CACCIATORA

I stood on the roof of a fortified farmhouse and looked across the acres of ancient olive trees that surrounded it to the plain and to the Adriatic Sea where warships, supply vessels and aircraft carriers stood off the coast of Brindisi, part of the seemingly hopeless war in Bosnia. In former times this tranquil part of Italy had been the scene of warring, religious feuding, banditry and rustling. From the time of the Moors and the Christians and the Saracens. The robber barons. The warlords and the Popes. So landowners built their farms into fortresses and with their walled gardens of lemon and orange trees and vineyards, with their olives, vegetables and livestock, they led a self-contained existence. Curing hams, making sausages and salamis, pressing the olives for oil and crushing grapes for wine, salting fish for the winter and hunting flesh and fowl in the centuries-old olive groves, they must have been a contented lot.

I certainly was on that spring morning as the azure sea sparkled in the sun, my rabbit sizzled in the pot and a breeze shimmered the leaves on the trees from sage and forest green to twinkling silver blades. You'll find my recipe over the page.

HUNTER'S RABBIT

CONIGLIO ALLA CACCIATORA

Serves 4

6 tablespoons olive oil
1 large onion, chopped
4 large rabbit joints (ask your
    butcher for the liver and
    kidneys too)
Salt
1 or 2 wineglasses of dry white
    wine (Italian, of course)

1 tablespoon chopped fresh
    parsley, flat-leaf if possible
2 tablespoons capers (use salted
    ones if you can get them, rather
    than ones pickled in vinegar)
Freshly ground black pepper
Chopped fresh parsley, to garnish
Crusty bread, to serve

Heat 4 tablespoons of the olive oil in a large flameproof casserole and fry the onion gently for about 5 minutes, until softened. Pop in the rabbit joints, add a good pinch of salt and fry for another 5 minutes over a moderate heat, turning the rabbit pieces to brown them all over. Put the lid on the casserole and turn the heat to low. Cook for 30 minutes.

Add the glass (or two) of wine and continue to cook for about 20 more minutes until the rabbit is tender. Just before the end of cooking time, heat the remaining olive oil in a small frying pan. Quickly chop the liver and kidneys and sauté them briskly for 2 minutes. Add to the cooking pot for extra flavour with the parsley, capers and some ground black pepper. Cook for 2 minutes, then serve with a good scattering of parsley on top and plenty of fresh, crusty bread.

PEASANT-STYLE STEW OF SIMMERED MEATS

BOLLITO

In moments of gastronomic despair I recall frequently the rumbustuous dishes that my mother and grandmother would prepare Saturday teatimes for that was the terminology in the fifties in Wiveliscombe. It might have been a pig's trotter soused in malt vinegar and seasoned with salt and pepper, whose little bones you sucked clean of flesh, or a whole boiled and pressed ox tongue served with home-made pickles and chutneys for Boxing Day evening or the vibrantly coloured, breadcrumb-coated pig's cheek known, as I remember, as a Bath Chap. Winter Mondays, when there was money, there was often a rich stew of flank of beef. Often – as I tuck into my roulade of sole and crab mousse in the front end of the plane where the inflight service director flatters me with extra wine – I think back to those days that many people would regard as the bad old days. For us there was no salmon, no sole (except in the cooking) while today the world's table, its kitchen and its cooks are at my disposal.

So can you imagine my delight when, after a brittle but sunny Alba autumn morning spent with a mongrel dog and a man with a stick looking for truffles, I was introduced to *Bollito*, a sumptuous dish made from tongues, trotters, spicy sausages, chicken, flank of beef and vegetables that had been simmered for several hours, filling the already perfumed country-side with the sensual odours of real peasant food. I was back to what I hope to be the future.

PEASANT-STYLE STEW OF SIMMERED MEATS

BOLLITO

Serves 12 or more

1 ox tongue
1 pig's cheek
900g (2lb) piece flank of beef, with bones
900g (2lb) shin of beef or veal
1.35–2kg (3–4½ lb) boiling chicken
3–4 onions, peeled
2 carrots, peeled
3–4 sticks of celery, scrubbed
Salt and freshly ground black pepper
1 bay leaf
900g (2lb) robust pork sausages, in one or two strings

DRESSING ONE
2–3 cloves of garlic, crushed
A handful of fresh parsley, flat-leaf if possible, finely chopped
Juice of 1 lemon
6 tablespoons olive oil
Salt and freshly ground black pepper

DRESSING TWO
2–3 cloves of garlic, crushed
4 tomatoes, skinned, seeded and chopped
2 pimentos, chopped (canned, drained pimentos are fine)
3 tablespoons wine or cider vinegar
6 tablespoons olive oil

To make the *Bollito*, bring a huge pot of water up to the boil. Add the ox tongue and simmer gently for about 1 hour, then add the pig's cheek and cook for another half an hour.

Add the flank of beef and the shin of beef or veal, the boiling chicken and the vegetables (which are left whole). Season with salt and ground black pepper, add the bay leaf, then cover and simmer for about 3½ hours.

Add the strings of sausages to the pot and simmer for another half an hour. When cooked, lift the meats out of the broth and slice them thinly. Serve on a huge plate with the dressings or with a pot of mustard, a pot of cold toma-to sauce and a pot of pesto (see the recipe for Red Mullet with Pesto).

To make each dressing, just put the ingredients into small bowls and whisk together well.

The sausages sold over the bar at my modest emporium – 'Floyd's Inn (Sometimes)' – are popular and they are very good and made by my butcher at Bridgetown in Totnes. They are chunky, traditional pork sausages, girt big 'uns. Long live the British Sausage. Long live Bridgetown.

It is very simple.

You need (and there are no exact measurements in this recipe):

A good old-fashioned hand-operated mincer – not an electric machine – with a sausage tube attachment

A length of hog's or sheep's casings – sausage skins – which you should be able to get from your local butcher, especially if they make their own sausages

A quantity of leg and shoulder of pork. Two-thirds leg to one-third shoulder

But. But. I now know how to make Italian sausages: fresh to grill or fry or cured to slice and eat with olives, bread and wine. I learned at a farmhouse high in the hills in Calabria.

A load of crushed, not ground, black peppercorns

A *soupçon* of dried fennel seeds

A handful or more of fine quality paprika and some salt

Grind the pork coarsely in the mincer. Chuck it into a large bowl, add the peppercorns, fennel seeds, paprika and salt. Mix together really well with your hands. Now fix the sausage tube attachment and sausage casings to the mincer. Then put the ground pork mixture back through the mincer and stuff the skins. Use some string to tie off the sausages and either hang them up to dry in a cool airy place to make salami or fry and grill them as normal. If you hang them up for three or four weeks they will keep for ages.

Note: In Italy they use pig's intestines for sausage skins, which are not allowed by the EC, but are easily available everywhere apart from Britain.

And now the politically incorrect caption:
'What's for lunch, luv?'

For the farmer who has everything. A Lamborghini tractor. He probably goes to market in a Ferrari.

A furry-purriness taking comfort from the store of winter warmth.

EC? What EC? Only the UK has the gall to interfere with the traditional mores of country folk. Preserves and the Women's Institute must be preserved at all costs. Try telling the Italians they have to conform to the absurd rules that are squeezing the life blood out of British small butchers and farmers and fishermen. Not to mention the cheesemakers.

'In a hut of clay and wattles made …'

'O fortunatos nimium, sua si bona norint, agricolas'
Which roughly translated, as I am sure you are aware, means 'the farmer's lot is a happy one.'

Have a break.

Every word hammered on
the anvil of truth.

WILD BOAR STEW
CINGHIALE STUFATO

As one who has eaten cobra in Saigon, crocodile in the Northern Territories, one-thousand-year-old eggs in Hong Kong and thrushes in Provence (a noted New Year's Eve delicacy), and as one who feels no guilt about despatching a lobster or preparing a crab, I have freely to admit that I have no conscience about hunting. Although I understand that for many this is a disagreeable pastime, it is a sad fact that those who protest against what is not only a natural rural pursuit but also a meaningful source of food do not possess the wit of Oscar Wilde, he being the one who described (fox) hunting as the unspeakable in full pursuit of the uneatable.

However, in Italy hunting for wild boar, hare, wild duck (I don't have many heroes but Hemingway is one and his evocative passages of wild duck hunting in Italy in the winter as indeed his allegorical sketches of trout fishing in Spain still leave me thrilled, envious and hungry) or truffles and mushrooms is not only a way of life, but a necessary part of everyday life. And in case you think I am being a pompous windbag, what I'm actually saying is this, that a country like Britain that throws bricks through the window of a shop selling any kind of animal-based material or that tries to stop people on crisp autumn days from galloping over fields and meadows is surely missing something. This is just not so in Italy. Sure, it is true that people say there is so much lead shot flying in the air from 12 and 20 bores that the hapless bird will just fly into it and crash to the ground, but if this is the way life has to be and the happiness of a nation is reflected by the sunshine on its plates then so be it. No self-respecting Italian will forsake his wild mushrooms, his pigeon, his truffle or his home-produced tomato sauce for the crap from the supermarket. When I was a boy gathering blackberries, watercress from the brooks, rising early to pick mushrooms or spending frozen hours on the snow-clad Somerset fields with a ferret, a net, a Thermos flask and a cheese doorstep sandwich were a way of life. Italy still has it, England doesn't.

In autumn in Italy game is the business. Wild boar is a fine meat to be served with sautéed chestnuts, peaches stewed in sweet white wine … Perfect for the season of mists and mellow fruitfulness.

WILD BOAR STEW
CINGHIALE STUFATO

Serves 6

1 leg of wild boar, cut into large
    pieces, or use about 1kg (2¼lb)
    leg of pork or venison
¾ bottle decent Italian red wine –
    we used La Suvera Rango 1988
2–3 bay leaves
Sprigs of fresh rosemary
Sprigs of fresh sage
2–3 cloves of garlic

1 carrot, cut into dice
2 red onions, peeled and quartered
6 tablespoons olive oil
Salt and freshly ground black
    pepper
300ml (½ pint) fresh tomato
    sauce or use passata or other
    prepared tomato sauce
Another wineglass of red wine

Put the pieces of meat into a large non-aluminium bowl and pour in the wine. (Keep the rest of the bottle for later.) Add the bay leaves, rosemary, sage, garlic, carrot and onions. Cover and leave in a cool place or refrigerate for 24 hours, so that the meat absorbs the flavours.

Next day, heat the olive oil in a large cooking pot. Add the meat, cooking it over a high heat to seal and brown it on all sides. Add some salt and freshly ground black pepper, then pour in the marinade. Stir in the tomato sauce and add another glass of red wine for good measure. Cover and cook in a preheated medium oven, 180°C/350°F (gas mark 4), until the meat is very tender. This should take about 2-2½ hours. Fish out the bay leaves.

Serve the Wild Boar Stew with vegetables fried in olive oil and peaches simmered in sweet wine and brown sugar.

BABY ONIONS

Cover with boiling water and soak for 5 minutes to make peeling easier. Peel them, then fry in olive oil with lemon juice and salt. Cook until they are golden brown and softened.

CELERY

Discard the coarse outer stalks, trim the celery and cut the hearts in half. Blanch for 3–4 minutes in boiling salted water. Drain well, then fry in olive oil.

CARROTS

Cut into quarters lengthways and cook as for celery.

PEACHES

Halve and stone 3 large peaches, blanch in boiling water then poach in sweet wine, such as Vin Santo, the juice of half a lemon and 50g (2oz) soft brown sugar. Simmer gently until soft.

CHESTNUTS

Bring to the boil in a pan of water, then allow them to cool in water. Peel off the outer and inner skins, then fry in olive oil until lightly coloured.

ITALIAN HERB OMELETTE

Serves 6

The *frittata*, or open omelette, is as good served cold as hot or warm. It is cooked until set firm and makes excellent picnic food or an addition to a platter of antipasti as well as a light lunch or supper. Rewardingly versatile, *frittate* can be made very successfully with artichokes, asparagus, courgettes, mushrooms or fennel, as well as the humble onion or potato.

This version, with a simple mixture of heady herbs, is especially summery. Beat 6 large eggs with 1 tablespoon water. Add 25g (1oz) freshly grated Parmesan cheese and 50g (2oz) chopped fresh herbs, such as parsley, basil and chives, or marjoram, thyme and sage. Season with salt and freshly ground black pepper and stir well. Heat 2 tablespoons olive oil with 15g (½ oz) butter in a 25cm (10 inch) heavy-based non-stick frying pan until foaming, then pour in the egg mixture. Cook over gentle heat for 7–10 minutes until set underneath but still runny on top. Place under a preheated grill for 1–2 minutes until set on top. Loosen the edges of the *frittata* with a spatula, then slide on to a serving plate. Serve cut in wedges. A fresh tomato and basil sauce goes well with this.

CARPACCIO

I was told Carpaccio was invented at Harry's Bar in Venice. This is widely disputed. But Harry's Bar Carpaccio was a little disappointing. The thin slices of raw beef fillet were lightly drizzled with a fairly insipid cheese dressing. My version (he adds modestly) is superior.

Serves 4

350g (12oz) piece of beef fillet, well-chilled
4 tablespoons extra virgin olive oil
2 tablespoons lemon juice

Salt and freshly ground black pepper
Rocket leaves, to garnish
Razor-thin slices of Parmesan cheese

Make sure that your piece of beef is extremely cold – this makes it easier to slice – then slice it very thinly with a very sharp knife. Place a little pile of meat on 4 serving plates. Then, quite simply, mix together the olive oil and lemon juice, drizzle it over the meat and sprinkle with some salt and freshly ground black pepper.

Arrange some rocket leaves on each plate, then scatter the thin shavings of Parmesan cheese over the top of the meat. Simple, refreshing, delicious.

Beef and Mushrooms in Rubesco Wine

MANZO E FUNGHI IN VINO

Autumn in Umbria. The time of the year for the wine harvest and that gradual shift from warm sunny days to cool nights and crisp misty mornings. The time of hard work and anxiety to gather the harvest before the weather breaks and the time of great excitement because the Italians are potty about gathering wild mushrooms.

This dish is perfectly suited to autumn. Certainly, the headman from the Torgiano vineyards thought it splendid. You could serve it with fresh home-made pasta.

Serves 4

3–4 tablespoons olive oil

675g (1½ lb) chump or braising steak, cut into large chunks

Salt and freshly ground black pepper

450ml (¾ pint) Rubesco wine, or use good quality Italian red wine

300ml (½ pint) fresh tomato sauce (see page 82), or you could use 300ml (½ pint) passata or prepared tomato sauce

Few sprigs of fresh sage and parsley

2–3 cloves of garlic, unpeeled

About 50g (2oz) of fat cut from Parma ham, diced into small cubes

350g (12oz) wild mushrooms, or use good flavoured mushrooms such as ceps or chestnut mushrooms, roughly chopped

Chopped fresh sage and parsley, to garnish

Heat the olive oil in a large frying pan and add the meat, sealing and browning it over a high heat. Season it with salt and black pepper. Transfer the meat to a casserole dish, adding a little more olive oil. Pour in the wine and add the tomato sauce. Pop in the sage, parsley and garlic cloves. Cover and cook over a low heat or in a preheated oven, 180°C/350°F (gas mark 4), for 1½ hours, or until the beef is really tender.

Towards the end of cooking time, sauté the fat from the Parma ham to render it down. Add the mushrooms and sauté them briskly for 4–5 minutes. Season with some salt and pepper and add a good pinch of chopped fresh sage and parsley. Add to the beef stew, stir well and serve.

BEEF AND MUSHROOMS IN RUBESCO WINE
MANZO E FUNGHI IN VINO

Note: Because wine is very cheap in Italy another method of preparing this dish is as follows:

Brown the chunks of meat in olive oil in a large sauté pan. Cover the meat with wine, season with salt and pepper and add a tablespoon of tomato purée or chopped fresh tomatoes. Turn up the heat to maximum and boil away the wine till the meat is dry again. Then add more wine and boil that fiercely. Repeat this 3 or 4 times over the period of about 1 hour; by then the meat will have taken on a very strong, rich wine flavour but will still not be cooked. So now re-cover the meat with wine, add the sage, parsley and garlic cloves, pop the lid on the pot and simmer until tender. Then proceed as in the method on the previous page.

Autumn and mushroom mania grips Italians like a fever. Hedgerows, forests, copses and fields rustle under the basket-bearing invasion of mushroom-gatherers. Who pluck, gather and sniff their quarry before placing it with reverence in the basket. And take the mushrooms carefully home to sauté with eggs or immerse in rich stews. Or grill naturally over a charcoal fire while they sip soft red wine before the open fire …

The cep, sometimes known as Penny Bun, is one of the most important edible mushrooms. It is widely sold in dried form.

Wood blewitts, bluish-lilac at
first, becoming brown, are
common and excellent to eat.

FRIED WILD MUSHROOMS

Serves 4–6

Beat 4 eggs and season well with
salt and freshly ground black pepper. Dip about 1kg (2¼lb) wild
mushrooms (or use a variety of
good flavoured mushrooms such
as ceps or chestnut mushrooms),
which you have wiped, in the egg
and coat with 100g (4oz) dried
breadcrumbs. Heat some olive oil
in a large frying pan and gently
fry the mushrooms until golden,
turning them occasionally.
Serve with lemon wedges.

Note: Mushrooms can be
hard to identify and edible
ones can easily be confused
with poisonous ones.
You must be sure of the
type of mushroom before
cooking and eating it.

MIXED MUSHROOMS WITH TOMATO

Serves 4–6

Heat 5 tablespoons of olive oil in a large frying pan. Add 1 finely chopped onion and sauté until transparent, about 3–4 minutes. Stir in a large tomato, which you have skinned, seeded and chopped, together with 2 bay leaves and a sprig of fresh rosemary. Cook for a couple of minutes, then add 750g (1¾lb) mixed wild mushrooms, which you have wiped and roughly chopped. Continue to cook over a low heat for about 20 minutes, stirring every now and again. Season with some salt and freshly ground black pepper, take out the bay leaves, then serve.

Caesar's mushroom thrives in warm climates, in deciduous woodlands, and is delicious to eat.

HOT HORSE
MUSHROOMS

Serves 4–6

Arrange 4–8 horse mushrooms
(that is, large, round and flat
ones), which you have wiped and
removed the stems from, gills
uppermost, in a shallow heatproof
dish. Finely chop 3 cloves of garlic
and sprinkle over the mushrooms,
together with 3 tablespoons of
chopped fresh parsley and 2–3
seeded and finely chopped small
fresh red chillis. Drizzle over 3–4
tablespoons of extra virgin olive
oil and pop under a preheated
hot grill for about 10 minutes.
Serve immediately.

Truffles.
More precious than diamonds.
Grated with surgical precision
on to risottos and pasta. Or
stored with fresh eggs to infuse
them with the exquisite aroma.

Soft-eared mongrel dogs dig
excitedly but gently for the black
or white gold. The white Italian
truffle is more esteemed than the
black. While puppies the dogs
are fed on truffles till they
become 'addicted'. Then straight
into 'cold turkey'. But the
hounds have an incurable desire.
To the woods. To the woods.

It takes a lot of time and money to produce a nose like this. He was offered a job by Dior, but why waste your time sniffing things you can't eat? Or drink for that matter.

Cursèd be the factories.
For though they produce cheese
and jobs and money
They give no joy
To the cheese-eater.
And I am a cheese-eater.
Are the men in white hats?

High in the Calabrian mountains between the Tyrrhenian Sea and a strange drab town called Castrovillari (but which has a most agreeable hotel called the President Jolli where they actually cook good food), there is an old farm. It has crumbled into disrepair and La Mamma (I don't know her name) and her three middle-aged bachelor sons keep goats, sheep and cattle. They also make cheese in the old way, in slow-simmering pans hung over a wood fire in a crumbling stone-built shed. This stands next to the chicken run and looks across the dried-up, pebble-filled riverbed wending its waterless way to the sea.

Goats and cows.
Sheep and buffalo.
Lovingly tended.
Milked by hand.

A fire of olive wood burns under an old cauldron full of simmering milk. Gnarled old hands stir and form the cheeses, without gloves, thermometers, clocks and stainless steel. A lifetime of love ends up in your tummy as you munch a plate of cheese.

With a stick of celery.
A slice of bread.
A spring onion.
Or a glass of wine.
Blessèd be the cheesemakers.

And on this merry Sunday morning the wind howled and hustled the March clouds across the sky while Mamma was making cheese. I had half a pig left over from my sausage-making sequence and I asked her if I could roast it over her fire once the cheesemaking had been completed. Yes, she said.

I gathered thyme from the hillside and stuffed the pig with that fine herb plus rosemary, crushed garlic, salt-sweet Sicilian lemon juice and black pepper. Then I bound it up with some rusty old wire from a derelict farm fence and set it to cook over the apple and olive wood fire.

Four hours and several palpitations later I offered the succulent crisp pork to the film crew. Mamma and her sons had departed for a funeral.

And it is not just the produce that makes shopping and eating such a pleasure. The shop fronts and restaurant windows are alluringly designed and decorated. I could no more walk past without entering this chocolate shop in Cherasco or this trattoria near Lake Maggiore than I could walk past a pub in the Sahara Desert.

When Sue Lawley asked for my luxury item on *Desert Island Discs* I requested a cheese shop. She refused. So I settled for a hamper of the following:

Gorgonzola; Mozzarella; Taleggio; Robiola; Taleggino; Robiolina; Stracchino; Pannerone; Mascarpone; Asiago; Fontina; Pecorino; Ricotta; and Provola.

Now this little list of delicious cheeses (and if only one kind of food was permitted in the entire world and I had to choose it would be cheese) in England would involve a sterile spin with a shiny trolley under the floodlights of a supermarket collecting packaged portions while having your ankles bruised by

A hand-made Venetian mask.
Designed originally to enable
libertine Italians to flirt and
commit adultery with an easy
conscience at outrageous balls
and parties. I bought one to
hang on my wall. That's life,
I suppose.

desperate shoppers shouting at
their kids as they blindly career
around clasping shopping lists
and checking prices. In Italy the
shopkeeper is an artist. And the
customer is a passionate patron.
In Italy shopping is a way of life.

PIEDMONTESE CHEESE FONDUE
FONDUTA

Fonduta is one of the classic dishes of Piedmont. It is important not to confuse it with a Swiss fondue, which uses wine or cider. Normally the dish is prepared with Fontina cheese, a mild, semi-soft, creamy cow's milk cheese, which is similar to Gruyère. But, if you wanted, you could make it from a mixture of cheeses to vary the flavour or even a Dutch Edam. When your stomach needs a rest from rich food or meat, this is a perfect alternative.

Serves 4

350g (12oz) Fontina cheese, cut into small pieces
600ml (1 pint) milk
4 eggs, beaten

75g (3oz) butter, cut into dice
Salt and freshly ground black pepper
2–3 white truffles, finely sliced

Put the cheese into a bowl with the milk and leave it for approximately 4 hours, so that the milk is partially absorbed.

Pour the cheese and milk mixture into a double saucepan. Add the eggs and butter. Season with salt and ground black pepper and heat, stirring continuously with a small whisk.

When the mixture has combined into a smooth, creamy consistency, which will take about 20 minutes, pour it into an earthenware serving dish and scatter the slices of white truffles (white gold) over the top. Dunk in chunks of fresh bread to eat.

Note: As it stands, eating the *Fonduta* with the cubes of fresh bread and a glass of red wine makes a superb light lunch or supper. But the version I had at the Trattoria della Posta was lifted to magnificence by the addition of a soft poached free-range egg plopped into each portion with a liberal shaving of white truffle scattered over the whole dish.

None other than Leonardo da Vinci once said, 'I believe much happiness descends upon those born where good wines are to be found.' I wasn't born in Italy, but when I was there I did have a very happy time trying out the wines. With the help of my local wine merchant, I've compiled what I hope will be these useful notes.

Italy produces what is perhaps the most diverse range of wines in the world and this tremendous variety reflects the country's geography; from the mountains of the Alps to the scorched lands of the far south.

Traditional grape varieties are now vinified with modern techniques and the old criticisms that Italian whites were flat and that the reds lacked fruit are simply no longer true. The classic French varieties – Chardonnay, Cabernet Sauvignon et al – have been planted alongside, and are often blended with, the home-grown Sangiovese, Nebbiolo, Trebbiano and Montepulciano. Cabernet Sauvignon and Sangiovese together, for example, can create a more finely structured and elegant red wine than could be made from Sangiovese alone.

The diversity of Italian wine is at once its delight and its confusion. Italian wine laws (DOC, or *Denominazione di Origine Controllata*, which is akin to the French '*appellation contrôlée*') have become so out of line with the revolution taking place in the vineyards that some of the finest new-wave wines are classified as mere table wine. These wines have to rely on their reputation and stylish names.

I hope that the best of the wine-making traditions will be preserved and the more questionable ones will fall by the wayside (too much exposure to oak, raw tannins and a lack of fruit). It would not be a good thing if Italy ended up producing bland 'international' wines from nothing but the ubiquitous Chardonnay and Cabernet.

Here are my favourite wine-growing areas, from north to south:

TRENTINO-ALTO ADIGE –
The two main DOCs from this region are Alto Adige, whose high vineyards and cool climate produce German-style white wines, and Trentino to the south, which is better known for its reds. The delicious white Bolzano also comes from here.

PIEDMONT – The reds of Piedmont are among Italy's greatest and the best come from the Nebbiolo grape, which is used to make the gutsy and, when aged, the gloriously brick-red Barolo, Barbaresco and the lesser Gattinara. The white wines include the ubiquitous sparkling Asti Spumanti and Moscato d'Asti, both made from the Moscato grape.

LOMBARDY – This region also produces some fine Nebbiolo reds, especially the DOC of Valtellina.

VENETO – Two of Italy's best-known and most widely drunk wines, Soave and Valpolicella, are grown here. These wines may be nothing special but they are usually reliable and good value – buy the Classico if you can.

EMILIA-ROMAGNA – By far and away the most famous wine from this region is the slightly sparkling and quaffable Lambrusco – drink very chilled.

FRIULI – Home of Silvio Jermann, one of Italy's great white winemakers, who uses both traditional and modern grape varieties to make a number of wines, including Collio, one of the best in the area.

TUSCANY – Tuscany produces not only Chianti Classico – which at its best is very good indeed – but also the more exotic and expensive Brunello di Montalcino and Vino Nobile di Montepulciano. The best of these stand comparison with the top clarets from Bordeaux.

MARCHES – Known for the brilliantly clear, slightly bitter white Verdicchio.

UMBRIA – The lovely Orvieto is produced here, mainly from the Trebbiano grape, and is either dry or, more traditionally, semi-sweet (*abboccato*).

LATIUM – Home to the very popular Frascati and the memorably named 'Est, Est, Est'.

CAMPANIA – From this region on the south-west coast comes Lacrima Christi, which is grown on the volcanic slopes of Mount Vesuvius and also on the island of Ischia. The wine takes its name from a legend – God, on the seventh day of creation, was so moved by the sight of the Bay of Naples that He shed a tear, which became the vine on which the Lacrima Christi grape is now grown. So now you know.

SICILY – Although the South is a bigger producer of wine than the North, its wines are not so well known; the best of them probably come from Sicily. Corvo is widely exported (the red is far superior to the white). For something classier try Regaleali. Marsala, the sweet fortified wine of Sicily, is used a great deal in Italian cooking (see pages 166–70).

All kinds of macerated fruit are popular in Italy – thinly sliced oranges, for example, arranged in layers sprinkled with sugar, lemon and orange zest, a little chopped mint and fresh orange juice or orange liqueur. They should be served really chilled. Peaches, either golden-yellow or the less common *pesca bianca*, grow abundantly in southern Italy and are often served poached or simply macerated in Moscato, sweet white dessert wine.

Robust red wine, such as Chianti, goes beautifully with pears. Choose 6 firm pears with the stalks on. Dissolve 175g (6oz) caster sugar in 725ml (1¼ pints) red wine in a large, heavy-based saucepan, and add a few strips of orange zest and a cinnamon stick. Peel the pears, leaving the stalks on, and cut a small slice from the base of each so that they stand up right. Place in the red wine mixture, pour in boiling water to come to the tops of the fruit, cover and cook over gentle heat until tender (about 15–20 minutes). Remove from the heat and leave the pears to cool in the wine for several hours, turning them occasionally to ensure an even crimson colour. Carefully transfer to a serving dish. Remove the zest and cinnamon from the wine mixture and boil for 5–10 minutes until reduced to a syrupy consistency. Pour over the pears and leave to cool, then chill for 1 hour. Serve with creamy Mascarpone cheese.

There is nothing more gratifying or pleasing to the tired eyes of a world-weary travelling cook than the sight of a well-stocked bar. In Italy bar design is lifted to an art form. Many of the bottles used for liqueurs and grappas are hand-blown and designed by serious craftsmen.

PS Some of the best grappas are produced by Jacopo Poli.

Here's another one of me at the
Trattoria della Posta, Monforte,
near Alba, where I lunched on
the most superb *Fonduta* with
poached egg and white truffle.

On the day of my visit Harry's Bar in Venice was full of Americans drinking coffee. It seemed to me not only had Hemingway's ghost departed but his spirit also.

This is a real labour of love –
truly hand-made spaghetti. For
three hours she serenely and
rhythmically rolled each individ-
ual length of spaghetti by hand.

As with bars no expense is
spared on equipment for the
Italian kitchen. The kitchens I
visited were efficient, bustling,
cheery places. To my delight,
instead of the dour-faced,
humourless chefs and plump,
pale-faced, frightened commis
one sees so often, these kitchens
were staffed with vivacious yet
practical women, the veritable
culinary sisters of mercy.

I started my curious culinary
career at the greasy sink of a
Bristol coffee bar. It is an
essential stage of training for all
those who work in the hospitality
industry. If you don't want to try
it first-hand may I recommend
George Orwell's *Down and Out
in Paris and London.*

'Get out of that bed and rattle
those pots and pans ...'

Letting it all hang out.

When I'm in chauvinistic (British) mood I take great delight in reminding Spanish and Portuguese friends that the Brits invented sherry, port and Madeira. They also invented that excellent apéritif or after-dinner dessert wine called Marsala, which comes from the Sicilian port of the same name. In many ways similar to sherry, this fortified and usually sweet wine is traditionally aged in oak barrels for up to twelve years and can be as strong as 18°.

Sip a glass of Marsala with
crystallised fruits, dates and
nuts – it is brilliant.

Sip a glass of Marsala before
lunch – most titillating.

Bubble a glass of Marsala into the pan juices after you have sautéd an escalope of veal.

SALTIMBOCCA, MY WAY

Serves 6

25g (1oz) plain flour
6 very thin escalopes of veal
6 very thin slices of Parma ham
6 large scampi tails, shelled
6 fresh sage leaves
Juice and finely grated zest of
  1 lemon
Salt and freshly ground black
  pepper
100g (4oz) butter
6 large scampi, whole
1 wineglass of dry Marsala
300ml (½ pint) single cream
2 tablespoons chopped fresh
  parsley

Sprinkle flour over the slices of veal. Use a rolling pin to beat them flat. On to each piece of veal place one slice of Parma ham, one scampi tail and a leaf of sage. Add a squeeze of lemon juice and sprinkle with pepper. Roll up each one tightly and secure with a couple of wooden cocktail sticks. Melt half the butter in a frying pan and sauté the veal rolls gently, turning them every now and again until golden – about 15 minutes. Squeeze over a little more lemon juice. Remove the veal rolls and keep them in a warm place.

Add half the remaining butter to the pan and fry the whole scampi for 2–3 minutes. Add more lemon juice and season with salt and pepper. Now add the Marsala and let this reduce for about 5 minutes. Remove the scampi and arrange them on a warm plate with the veal rolls.

Add the cream and remaining butter to the juices left in the pan. Heat gently, stirring constantly. When the butter has melted, the sauce is ready to pour over the scampi and veal. Serve at once, garnished with the lemon zest and chopped parsley.

ZABAGLIONE

Whisk Marsala with egg yolks and sugar for a frothy dessert or, indeed, a pick-me-up for those under the weather – Zabaglione!

This is simple to make but quite hard work. Your whisking hand needs to be in good shape.
For each person you need two big yellow egg yolks, a couple of tablespoons of caster sugar and a dash of Marsala.

First, whisk together the egg yolks and sugar, then put the mixing bowl over a pan of gently simmering water. Pour in the alcohol and whisk like hell until you have a smooth, frothy thick custard like mixture. Serve in glasses with sweet biscuits.

Just desserts.
Sun-drenched strawberries
and sweet oranges.
A perfect way to finish a
good meal.
Or if you have a sweet tooth
like me ...
Italian ice cream is the best
in the world.

Zuppa di Inglese
is a great cake.

ZUPPA DI INGLESE

Serves 4–6

FOR THE CUSTARD
3 eggs, plus 1 egg yolk
50g (2oz) caster sugar
2 tablespoons cornflour
900ml (1½ pints) milk
2 strips of lemon zest

FOR THE REST
50g (2oz) dark chocolate
A few drops of red food
    colouring
A plain Madeira cake, sliced
4 tablespoons Marsala
3 tablespoons Amaretto di
    Saronno

Beat together the eggs, egg yolk and sugar and put them into a saucepan. Blend the cornflour with 3 or 4 tablespoons of the milk and add it, with the remaining milk, to the saucepan. Add the strips of lemon zest. Heat this mixture gently, stirring it all the time with a wooden spoon, until it just boils and thickens. Don't heat it too rapidly or else you will end up with scrambled eggs. Remove the lemon zest and divide the custard equally between two jugs.

Melt the chocolate over a pan of gently simmering water, then mix it into one of the jugs of custard. Add the red food colouring and mix well.

Put the slices of cake in a large serving bowl. Mix together the Marsala and Amaretto, pour over the cake and let them soak in. Now take the jugs of custard and pour over some of the plain custard and some of the chocolate-flavoured. Repeat this until both lots of custard are used up. Cover the dish and chill it in the fridge for at least a couple of hours.

Both divine inspiration.

'Did you hear the one about ...'

Salvador Dali said that
cake-making and architecture are
two of the greatest art forms.

Ferrara Cathedral.

Orvieto Cathedral.

Life in the fast lane.
For those who have time to
    stand and stare.
And talk of former times.
And future meals
Of wild mushrooms
Or pasta with grated white
    truffles.

Life in the fast lane.
For those not condemned to
    old people's homes
Who have time to talk of football
    and Ferraris
Or of crime and punishment.
Or Bishops,
Popes
Or politics.

Fiat on a hot tin roof.

Historians and archaelogists are undecided about the origins of these curious *trulli* houses in Apulia, but you can take it from me that this is where the trolls live.

The Greek temple at Segesta. The cultural head of Sicily refused to allow me to cook here. A pity, I needed some divine inspiration.

INDEX